GOATS

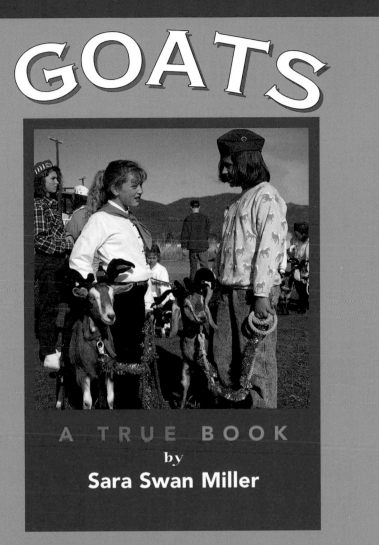

A TRUE BOOK

by
Sara Swan Miller

Children's Press®
A Division of Grolier Publishing
New York London Hong Kong Sydney
Danbury, Connecticut

A hungry goat

Reading Consultant
Linda Cornwell
Coordinator of School Quality
and Professional Improvement
Indiana State Teachers Association

Content Consultant
Jan Jenner

Visit Children's Press® on the Internet at:
http://publishing.grolier.com

Library of Congress Cataloging-in-Publication Data

Miller, Sara Swan.
    Goats / by Sara Swan Miller.
        p.   cm. — (A True book)
    Includes bibliographical references (p.   ) and index.
    Summary: Describes the physical traits, lifestyle, and behavior of goats
and their role in providing humans with milk.
    ISBN 0-516-21578-7 (lib. bdg.)   0-516-27182-2 (pbk.)
    1. Goats Juvenile literature.   [1. Goats.]   I. Title. II. Series
SF383. 35 .M55   2000
636. 3 ' 9—dc21   99-30139
                                                          CIP

Contents

These goats are grazing in a field in Norway.

The Goat Story

Have you ever seen goats running and jumping about on a farm? Do you know why farmers keep them? Did you know that they give milk, like cows? In fact, around the world more people get their milk from goats than from cows.

Milking a goat

Goat milk is easier to digest than cow milk. Goats are easier to raise, too. They can survive in mountains and dry places where cows cannot. They can eat things that cows won't. Because they are small, they also eat less and take up less room. Some people call goats "the poor person's cow."

People in Asia tamed wild goats more than nine thousand years ago. People in

These goats find their food in a dry mountain region.

The top row of this ancient Egyptian wall painting shows a farmer leading a goat by its horn.

ancient Egypt raised goats, also. Goats have lived with people longer than any other animal except dogs.

Over the years, people bred the best goats together to make many different breeds, or kinds, of goats. Some breeds give more milk.

This pigmy goat has been specially bred for its meat and milk.

Others give richer milk. Some are grown for their wool. Still others are raised for their meat. Now there are more than 210 breeds of goats.

A Toggenburg goat

Some Favorite Breeds

Toggenburg goats are small,
but they give a lot of milk.
They're good for farmers who
don't have a lot of room to
keep them.
La Mancha goats have almost
no ears at all! But they can
hear just fine. Their milk is
rich in butterfat.

Nubian goats have ears that hang down like a hound's. They are the most popular breed in the United States. Saanan goats are all white. These goats are strong and give a lot of good-tasting milk.

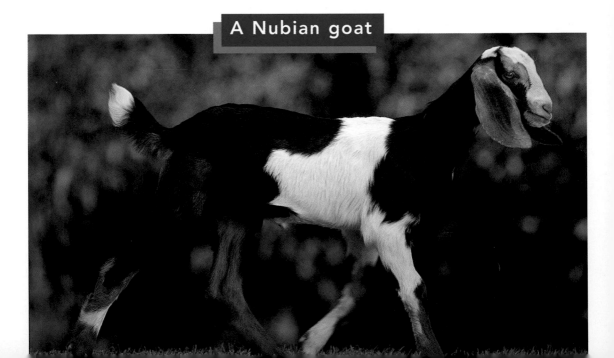

A Nubian goat

An Angora goat

People raise Angora goats for their wool. They are covered with long, silky hair called mohair. People knit it and weave it into soft sweaters and shawls.

Do Goats Eat Cans?

Some people say that goats eat anything, even tin cans and wood. But that isn't true. If you see a goat with a can, it's probably just licking off the glue that makes the label stick to the can. Or it may just be checking it out to see if there's something good to eat inside. Goats are very curious!

Even a wooden bench
can be tasty to a goat!

Goats have special physical features, such as pupils shaped like rectangles (inset) and a long beard.

What Are Goats Like?

If you have a chance to see a goat close up, one of the first things you may notice is its eyes. The pupils aren't round like the ones in your eyes. They're little rectangles. Many goats have beards hanging down from their chins. Goats have horns, too.

Both male and female goats have horns, but the male's horns are bigger.

Farmers usually remove the horns when the goats are very young, however. This doesn't hurt the goat. A goat with horns might hurt some-one by mistake or get its horns stuck in a fence.

Can you see some ways this sheep is different from a goat?

Do you know the difference between goats and sheep? Sheep have dense wool called fleece. Goats have hair, which makes them nice to pet. They sound different, too. Sheep say, "Baa," but goats say, "Maa." They even smell different. If you have ever smelled goat cheese, you have an idea of what goats smell like. They have a strong smell, a little like old milk. The males, or bucks, smell especially strong. But people who raise them like the smell.

In the summer, goats live outside. They like small plants, roots, nuts, and berries. But, unlike cows, they

These goats are helping to trim overgrown bushes around a patio.

don't eat much grass. Sometimes they will stand on their back legs to eat leaves from a small tree or strip off its bark. Goats eat so many things that people used to let a herd of them loose in a brushy area to clear it. Then people could plant crops there.

Goats return to a warm, dry barn.

In cold or wet weather, goats stay inside a barn. People feed them corn, oats, hay, roots, and other food.

Goats' mouths are perfect for eating tough plants. They have no front teeth on the top of their jaw. Instead, they have a tough pad. They have

A goat's mouth is well suited for tearing and grinding almost anything.

strong teeth on the front of their lower jaw. They grab plants between their teeth and the pad and tear them off. Then they grind their food between their back teeth, called molars.

Goats in this herd lie down to chew their cud.

Have you ever seen a goat lying down chewing? It looks as if it's chewing gum. It is really chewing its cud.

Goats have four-part stomachs. When a goat eats, it doesn't chew its food much at first. It just makes the food wet enough to swallow. The food goes into the first two parts of its stomach. When the goat is full, it brings up a wad of food and chews it well. Then the cud goes down into the third and fourth parts of its stomach to be digested.

Female goats, or does, store their milk in their udder. Their young, called kids, suck the milk out of two teats, or nipples, on the udder. Usually

A pigmy goat nurses its kids.

a doe has two kids at a time,
one for each teat.

A doe starts making milk
only after she has kids. The
kids nurse from her teats at
first. Then the farmer feeds

A farmer bottle-feeds a kid.

them milk from a bottle or a
pail. Soon they start eating
grown-up goat food. The kids
don't need all the milk their
mother makes. The farmer
milks out the rest. This is the

A mother goat, or doe, and its kid

milk that people drink. The doe keeps giving milk for months after the kids are born. She usually gives about 1 gallon (4 liters) a day. That's sixteen glasses of milk!

When they're born, kids weigh about 7 pounds (3 kilograms). Just minutes after birth, they can stand on their wobbly legs and begin to nurse. A few days later they're bouncing around and playing.

A feeding trough becomes a climbing toy for these kids.

All goats are very playful. The kids, especially, love playing together. They play tag and follow the leader. They even play king of the mountain. One kid climbs on a high place, and the others try to push it off and be on top themselves. Some farmers build special toys for them to climb on.

Goats used to be mountain animals, and they love climbing. You may see a kid standing on the backs of a group of does. You may even see one standing on top of the goat shed! Farmers who keep goats need to build high, strong fences to keep them inside. A goat can leap over a 5-foot (2-meter)-high fence! Goats are smart, too. They can even learn how to open a gate latch.

A goat may climb a tree in its search for plants to nibble.

These goats share a rock pile with friends.

Goats are gentle and fun to have around. They like following people about and playing with them. Better yet, they enjoy getting a good scratch behind the ears.

On this farm, goats are milked by machine or by hand.

Goat Milk

Some people think goat milk tastes funny. But that's probably because they have never tasted fresh goat milk.

Every morning and every evening, the does need to be milked. The farmer puts them up on a milking stand and ties them so they'll stand still.

Having some food to eat helps them stay quiet. On small farms, farmers milk by hand into a clean pail or jar. It feels good to the doe when her heavy udder is empty.

Goat milk soaks up smells like a sponge. The milking room needs to be very clean so the milk will smell and taste good. To keep the milk fresh, it needs to be strained and pasteurized (PASS-chur-eyezd) right away. The milk is

In a milking room, many goats are milked at the same time.

Small wheels of goat cheese

heated to just the right temperature to kill germs. Then it is stored in a refrigerator.

Goat milk is good tasting and good for you, too. But there are also many other things that can be made from it. Both cheese and cottage cheese can be made from goat milk. Even ice cream and sherbet can be made from goat milk!

Making butter from goat cream is a little harder. The

After the goats are milked,
there is time for play.

cream in goat milk doesn't rise to the top the way it does in cow milk. If the farmer adds a little cow milk, it will. Then the cream can be churned into butter.

Taste some goat milk yourself and find out why people say it's delicious!

Make Your Own Sherbet

How would you like to make sherbet from goat milk?

You need:
1 quart (1 liter) goat milk
1 cup (250 ml) sugar
1/2 cup (125 ml) corn syrup
Juice of 3 lemons
Pinch of salt

Besides dairy products, goats give us an icy lemon dessert treat.

Mix the milk, sugar, corn syrup, and salt together. Pour it into a loaf pan. Put it in the freezer. When it's partly frozen, stir in the lemon juice. Stir the mixture twice more while it's freezing to make it smoother. It should be ready in about two hours.

Serve some in a bowl and enjoy!

To Find Out More

Here are some additional resources to help you learn more about goats.

 **Books**

Fowler, Alan. **Woolly Sheep and Hungry Goats.** Children's Press, 1993.

Jeunesse, Gallimard. **Farm Animals.** Scholastic, 1998.

McPhail, David M. **Farm Morning.** Harcourt Brace, 1991.

Montgomery, Francis Trego. **Billy Whiskers: The Autobiography of a Goat.** Dover Publications, 1997.

Stevens, C.J. **One Day With a Goat Herd.** John Wade Publishing, 1992.

Webster, Charlie. **Farm Animals.** Barron's, 1997.

Organizations and Online Sites

Breeds of Livestock
*http://www.ansi.okstate.
edu/BREEDS/goats*

If you want to see pictures of many different breeds of goats and descriptions of each, this is the place to visit.

Goat Kingdom
*http://members.tripod.
com/~duhgoatman/
goatkingdom.htm*

Here you can find pictures and brief descriptions of goats at Goat Kingdom Farm, as well as links to other goat farms.

Goats (North Carolina Cooperative Extension Service)
*http://www.ces.ncsu.edu/
lenoir/staff/jnix/pubs/an.
workbook/goat.html*

This site has information and facts about goats. You can also hear a goat bleating.

Information Dirt Road
*http://www.ics.uci.edu/~
pazzani/4H/InfoDirt.html*

This site contains information on raising different kinds of farm animals, including goats.

Kids Farm
http://www.kidsfarm.com

Kids Farm is a lot of fun and educational, too. It is created by people who run a farm in the Colorado Rocky Mountains. It brings you real sights and sounds of animals on the farm.

National 4-H Council
*http://www.fourhcouncil.
edu*

This site will tell you about animal clubs and special interest activities for youth across the United States.

Important Words

butterfat the natural fat in milk, which can be made into butter

fleece a sheep's wool coat

milking stand a platform a goat is placed on for milking

pasteurization the process of killing germs by heating milk to the right temperature

pupil the black part of the eye that lets light travel through it

udder the baglike part of a goat that hangs down near its back legs; it contains the glands that produce milk

Index

(**Boldface** page numbers indicate illustrations)

Meet the Author

Sara Swan Miller has enjoyed working with children all her life, first as a nursery-school teacher, and later as an outdoor environmental educator at the Mohonk Preserve in New Paltz, New York. Now Ms. Miller is a full-time writer. She has written more than thirty books for children, including *Cows*, *Chickens*, *Goats*, and *Sheep*, in the True Books series.

Photographs ©: Art Resource, NY: 8 (Erich Lessing); BBC Natural History Unit: 24 (Richard Du Toit), 16 inset (Artur Tabor); Envision: 43 (Steven Needham), 38 (Brooks Walker); Peter Arnold Inc.: 9 (John Cancalosi), 2 (Manfred Danegger), 13 (J. Frebet/Bios), cover, 27 (Gerard Lacz), 7 (J. Newby/Bios); Photo Researchers: 40 (Rainer Berg/OKAPIA), 37 (Nigel Cattlin/Holt Studios International), 19 (Tim Davis), 10 (E. R. Degginger), 12 (Renee Lynn), 13, 30 (Tom McHugh), 32 (John Moss), 21 (G. Carleton Ray), 18 (Hans Reinhard/OKAPIA); Visuals Unlimited: 6 (D. Cavagnaro), 33 (John D. Cunningham), 1 (Mark E. Gibson), 16 (Arthur R. Hill), 15 (Bob Newman), 4 (Charles Preitner), 34 (John Sohlden), 22 (Brooking Tatum); Wildlife Collection: 28 (Dietrich Gehring), 23, 26 (John Tyson).